IMAGES OF ENGLAND

Trowbridge

For six centuries, The George was the focus of much of the social and commercial life of the town. In 1935 it is decorated for the Silver Jubilee of King George V; the inn was originally named after St George in the fourteenth century. In 1935 it still had the balustrading at the top, which was soon afterwards replaced by a solid parapet. The iron finials on the gables were also later to disappear.

IMAGES OF ENGLAND

Trowbridge

Michael Marshman
and
Ken Rogers

NONSUCH

First published 1997
This new pocket edition 2005
Images unchanged from first edition

Nonsuch Publishing Limited
The Mill, Brimscombe Port,
Stroud, Gloucestershire, GL5 2QG
www.nonsuch-publishing.com

British Library Cataloguing in Publication Data.
A catalogue record for this book is available from the British Library.

ISBN 1-84588-185-0

Typesetting and origination by Nonsuch Publishing Limited
Printed in Great Britain by Oaklands Book Services Limited

Contents

Acknowledgements

We have been researching, collecting material, writing and giving talks on Trowbridge for many years. In that time many people have given us pictures to add to our own family archives. In turn we have given many copies of photographs to Trowbridge Museum, the Wiltshire and Swindon Record Office and the Wiltshire Libraries Photographic Collection. For this book we have been fortunate in discovering several previously unknown albums and collections, the owners of which have very kindly given permission for reproduction. We extend our grateful thanks to Frances Bushell of Trowbridge, Bob Hallam of Trowbridge, Jean Morrison of Bratton, Philip Davis of Pensford, Michael Lansdown of Trowbridge, Miss M. Pearce of Trowbridge, Alan Crudge of Southwick and Brian Wickham of Bradford.

We would also like to acknowledge the help provided by Trowbridge Museum, the Wiltshire and Swindon Record Office and Wiltshire County Council Libraries and Heritage.

Appreciation must also be given to the photographers, both amateur and professional, who have taken the photographs which appear in this book. Some of them are known to us but many are not, and we thank them all and hope that they approve of the way their pictures have been used to illustrate the town which they all knew at various times.

Introduction

The town which we know as Trowbridge began as a small settlement overlooking a wide shallow river. In Saxon times there was a ford, the wooden bridge which gave the town its name and a small church. By the time of the Domesday Book in 1086, it was an average-sized agricultural settlement where cloth was woven in long huts for local use. Early in the twelfth century the future shape and history of the settlement was decided when the manor of Trowbridge and other estates passed to the de Bohun family, who made Trowbridge their main residence and centre of their estates. A castle was built and was first documented in 1139 when it was garrisoned on behalf of the Empress Maud and unsuccessfully besieged by King Stephen.

The attendance of tenants and others at various courts held at Trowbridge could have been a stimulus to urban growth and the right to hold a market and annual fair was granted in 1200; tradesmen and artisans were living in the community by 1243 and probably earlier. The castle now gave shape to the street plan, with the more prosperous residents on burgage plots in Fore Street (before the castle) with others living in Back (now Church) Street. This pattern remained, although the castle which caused it had largely disappeared by the early sixteenth century. The market grew and occupied an area outside the castle gates in what is now the top of Castle Street and the pedestrianised part of Fore Street. A new church was built on the far side of the market place on the site of the present Church of St James.

Much of the parish was agricultural, farmed on the open field system, with the urban area occupying only a small amount of land. As well as farmers there would have been a miller, tanners, butchers, bakers, corn dealers, shoemakers, a chandler, a fisherman, two innkeepers (at The George and The Swan) and alehouse keepers. Also, from before 1306, there were the spinners, weavers and fullers who began the staple industry of Trowbridge.

By the mid-fifteenth century, there were wealthy and prosperous clothiers and although Trowbridge never approached the eminence of Salisbury in the medieval cloth industry, it flourished, and many good houses, both stone and timber-framed were built. The late sixteenth and early seventeenth centuries saw uncertainties in the woollen industry which affected the fortunes of Trowbridge and its clothiers, while the Civil War caused some upset as two of the principal clothiers had Royalist sympathies, although the town was only on the fringe of any military action. Prosperity returned after the Restoration and planned developments took place at The Conigre and Duke Street, following on from linear housing such as that on Silver Street and Roundstone Street.

The late seventeenth and early eighteenth centuries were a time of great prosperity for local clothiers and for much of the town. Visible evidence remains in the elegant houses of The Parade and elsewhere, which show that on the edge of the Bath stone area the town was being created with both stone and brick replacing the earlier timber-framing. Non-conformity spread rapidly from an early Baptist congregation at Southwick, finding a receptive audience among the independently-minded artisans associated with all aspects of the cloth industry. The number and range of shops and trades grew and included attorneys, doctors, clock makers, barbers, jewellers and, a little later, a printer and bookseller. This eighteenth century prosperity was dependent upon the cloth trade and, like every town, Trowbridge had large numbers of poor who were reliant upon charity, the parish and the workhouse. Education was either paid for or provided through charity.

The period around 1800 saw great changes in the cloth industry which were to influence the town's development during the next 100 years. First water, then steam provided the power for the mechanisation which took the industry from homes and workshops to factories. Housing was needed for factory workers who had moved in from the surrounding villages and from 1820 onwards, terraces of two storey houses were built as the town expanded outwards. For a time in the 1830s and 1840s, Trowbridge was the most populous place in Wiltshire, overtaking the cathedral city of Salisbury before itself being overtaken by the fast growing railway town of New Swindon. The century saw many peaks and troughs in the cloth industry and at one point there were seventeen factories at work in the town centre and the number of shops and services increased greatly.

Only a few miles away, at Lacock, Fox Talbot invented the photographic negative in the 1840s and although there is no evidence to suggest that he took photographs of Trowbridge, there were soon to be others recording the events and people of the town. From the second half of the nineteenth century there is much pictorial evidence to support the written record of town development, celebrations, tragedies and the everyday life of quite ordinary people. Professional photographers such as Nightingale, the Wilkinsons and the Houltons recorded both people and places and their work is complemented by a host of amateurs, many unknown, who have wished to record scenes and events for the pleasure of themselves and others.

Ken Rogers and Michael Marshman have, with Michael Lansdown, been involved in compiling two previous books of old photographs of their home town. Since then many more photographs have been discovered and are published here for the first time. They show a world which changed out of all recognition in less than a hundred years, although many buildings remain little changed, to act as backdrops to the varied life of the townspeople. From the seemingly well-ordered and complacent world of Victoria's reign, the town was introduced to exciting new ideas of the new century, only to be overtaken by a world war which few understood and in which 308 of their sons were to die in previously unheard of places. The cloth industry contracted while engineering and food processing began to replace it. Trowbridge became the centre of local government in Wiltshire and thereby the county town, much to the amazement of many visitors. The photographs in this book record some of the important events but there are many more everyday scenes of people going about their normal business which, after all, is what life mainly consists of rather than a series of momentous happenings.

Many old photographs have appeared in our previous books and this means that some areas and themes of the town may appear under-represented as we do not have any other photographs of them. The woollen industry has been well-illustrated in the past and so has not been included in this volume. References in the text are made to illustrations in past books thus: *Trowbridge in Pictures* (TIP), *The Book of Trowbridge* (BoT), *Trowbridge in Old Photographs* (TOP).

One

Street Scenes and Buildings

The 1930s saw major council estates built above Shails Lane, now Seymour Road, and here at Longfield Road. In the background of this 1936 picture are the houses of Mortimer Street looking across to the tower of Trinity Church.

Over the years, many views have been taken of the upper part of Fore Street looking towards the Town Hall, which give good details of variations in buildings and occupancy. Both views shown here date from about 1893–98, the short period when Bowyers occupied the elaborate building which is now the Portman Building Society. In 1898 they amalgamated with another bacon curing firm, Paynes, shown on the right in the lower photograph, and moved their shop to that site. Also evident are the two shop fronts of Chettle, draper, and Dyer, chemist, on what is now the Midland Bank, while on the right is the Woolpacks Inn.

Two more examples of changing detail in this part of Fore Street; the older view at the top shows the last house on the right, gone in the lower view, while the Public Benefit Boot Company has become Lennards and the row of lamps removed. On the left it can just be seen that the shop front to the left of the Market Tavern has been brought forward to form Hilsers' jewellers shop. This is the only picture we have so far seen to show the petrol pump at the roadside.

Pre- and post- First World War photographs of the central part of Fore Street show little change in buildings but a greater volume of traffic in the later one, though still only one car. The horse-drawn transport of the Royal Horse Artillery from the Barracks was a familiar sight in the town. In the later picture the building then used by Hepworths, now a betting shop, has received its mock-Tudor timber-framing.

The building of the London Central Meat Company, later Baxters, shown to the right of the lower picture opposite has now gone, as have its lower neighbours pictured here. These were replaced by the present colourless buildings of the 1960s. For some decades the Houlton family were the chief photographers of the town, specialising in portraits and weddings.

In the lower picture on the opposite page are mostly buildings still familiar today, but the nearest gabled building on the left was altered in the 1930s. It was the well-known Smith and King's bakery, cake shop and cafe and is seen here in its original state in about 1930.

A splendid late Victorian view of the commercial centre of Trowbridge. Knee's corner store sold everything for the home and was housed in a timber-framed building which was demolished in 1936. The shop fronts which were later carefully removed housed a draper and a chemist. The Avon Brush factory features in the Trades and Industry section (see page 39) and their shop was in another timber-framed building which was rebuilt in 1928.

The George was the chief inn of the town for 500 years and, when pictured, still provided the venue for all the major dinners and dances of the area in its ballroom. A medieval inn, refronted in the eighteenth century with gables and upper windows added by the Victorians, it was the centre of Trowbridge social life.

The railings in front of the Capital and Counties (now the National Westminster) Bank have gone, as has the combined horse trough, drinking fountain and gas lamp which stood on the pavement. The butcher's shop is still without the very large 'GARLICK' sign shown in later photographs. The two men talking were well-known tradesmen; in the apron is Tom Kingham, a grocer whose shop was on the site of the Shires entrance from the Market Place, in the cap is George Coleman, insurance and house agent whose business occupied the site of the present Boots.

The top picture has been published before (*TIP* 6 and *BoT* 33) but is included again so that it can be compared with the one below, also by the artist W.W. Wheatley. Abraham Bowyer started his grocer's and baker's business in the fine old timber-framed building in 1819, and replaced it by the present one in about 1840. The lower drawing dates from after 1851 when the present National Westminster Bank building replaced the Georgian house shown in the earlier scene.

People could walk on the road in the days before the First World War and the trees on The Parade added to the idyllic scene. To the left are the square bay windows of No. 5 Fore Street, then occupied as shops by Govers, grocers, and Coles, florists. These windows were removed in 1911 when the building became the post office.

This is the opposite view to the last, taken, *c.* 1905. The building farthest to the right was refronted, as shown here, in 1875 to the design of William Smith, the Trowbridge architect. At this time it was occupied by J.W. Culverhouse, tobacconist and photographer. Next door was Randall, saddler and harness-maker.

This view of Silver Street in about 1880 shows The Limes, on the site of the Town Hall, and the two smaller houses which were replaced in 1886 by the building now occupied by Lloyds and Mackays.

Silver Street in the period just before the First World War, shows the building occupied by Eastmans and Dotesio and Todd, booksellers, stationers and printers, and, adjoining it, the projecting building replaced in 1932.

Busy scenes in Church Street in 1905 (above) and about fifty years later (below). The Hare and Hounds public house, on the right of the older picture, has just been demolished and in the later one, the site cleared for a nondescript building which now occupies it. Further along the gables have been removed from the former Co-operative Central Stores.

The caption on this postcard says 'Hilperton Road' but in fact Marlborough Buildings, on the right, have always been numbered in Roundstone Street. Polebarn House is seen as it was, until it became County Council property in 1920, with its cladding of ivy, its decorative balls and urns and the large cupola on the roof.

Roundstone Street in the late 1950s, seen from Polebarn House, presents a very similar appearance to that of today. The area to the left, still used for parking cars, was formerly the front garden of Rodney House until the road was drastically widened in 1937.

This is one of the few detailed pictures of buildings in The Conigre. It shows the tin Mission Room which stood behind the houses on the upper side of Upper Broad Street. It was erected by voluntary subscriptions in 1887.

The back view of the Coach and Horses public house and adjoining houses in Upper Broad Street, seen during the demolition of 1934. Behind them is the still intact north side of the street. Most of this soon went, but the large Georgian house to the right, which looks semi-derelict, in fact continued to house Diplock's Printing Works until it closed in 1956. The Conigre pump still stands in Lower Broad Street but the top, now in Trowbridge Museum, has been removed.

These cottages stood in Waldron Square, a group of houses near Westcroft at the lower end of British Row. It was in the right hand building that John Wesley first preached in Trowbridge on 17 September 1754.

Silverthorne's Court still runs from Roundstone Street to Duke Street, but the sites of the houses are now untidy wasteland. The houses nearest the camera in the 1950s must have been built soon after 1700 but were clearly raised at a later date to provide workshop space for weavers.

A few years before the First World War, two pairs of houses with flat roofs were built in Drynham Road and promoted as having roof gardens. One is seen in use while in the background is the roof of the group of weavers' cottages known to Lower Studleyites as the Ivy Houses.

The writer on the back of this card in 1905 thought it 'a funny one of the hospital', and it is true that it does not show the building, later The Clinic, too well. But it does provide a picture of the long-gone buildings at the other corner of The Halve.

This varied group of old houses stood in Hilperton Road, stretching from just below the present fire station at the left to opposite the entrance to The Halve on the right. Seen here in the 1960s, the whole site is now occupied by a roundabout and waste land adjoining.

A closer view of the lower end of the same row of buildings, c. 1905. The cottages on the right stood at the corner of The Halve.

Many pictures, taken for particular purposes, will show other details of interest in the background, as in the following four photographs. Above, recruits are drilling in the Park in the First World War, showing a coach house in what is now the yard of Colbourne Trophies.

A procession on The Parade gives us the only known detailed view of the buildings which, until 1913, stood to the right of Parade House.

In the background to a procession in Gasworks Lane (now 'Riverway') is a gabled building which was the parish workhouse of the eighteenth century, later clothier's workshops, and adjoining it nearer the camera, a dye house.

Recruits going to the station to catch a train to Devizes to join the Wiltshire Regiment in 1914. The picture gives a good view of the buildings on either side of the river below the Town Bridge.

These two snapshots were taken from a bedroom window, c. 1930. A feature, now almost forgotten, is the tall poles needed to carry the aerials for what were then called wireless sets. Without these no signals could be received. The cottages, shown end on in the lower picture, stood in the lane leading from the Dursley Arms to the railway bridge. Behind them is the field now occupied by Cherry Gardens and, on the right, the house then called Wiwurri.

Above, below and opposite above: These three views of Gloucester Road in the late 1930s show a residential development begun in the 1850s and completed in the 1890s. The road was one of a grid pattern of streets to the south of Newtown, built to provide housing for workers in the woollen mills. The later houses, top right, were built for wealthier occupants and culminated in the more prestigious Westbourne Road and Avenue Road. The shop, with the array of enamelled advertising signs was one of many corner shops which were incorporated in these nineteenth century housing developments.

Philip Isley & Co., Carpenters, Builders, Contractors, Merchants and Sanitary Engineers, Tugela, Trowbridge.

Tugela House was built in about 1900, taking its name from a battle in the Boer War. It stood at the lower end of Wicker Hill, about where Presto Print is now, and can be seen in *TIP* 4. This is the only known view of the workshop and showroom part.

This scene of activity shows the beginning of building on the Longfield estate in 1936. The road is being made, using a steamroller, while a number of houses have been started. In those days scaffolds were still made of wooden poles roped together.

A much later stage in the building of the Longfield estate. The houses in Coronation Street are nearly complete, and in the foreground are seen the early stages in the construction of the Bathing Pool, opened in 1939.

As the two main public buildings in Trowbridge, the Market House built in 1861 and the Town Hall in 1887–89, stand next to one another, the area has been much photographed, and this enables us to devote a whole sequence to illustrate the development of Market Street. The story begins in 1861 when the Market House was opened, and the leading townspeople promised William Stancomb, who had provided it, that a road would be made in front of the building through to Castle Street. Nothing was done for many years, however. The first photograph in the series dates from before about 1881. It shows the Market House viewed from Fore Street, with the house on the corner of that street, No. 36, just showing at the right. The picture suggests that the roadway continued beyond, but in fact just out of sight stood the little building shown below. It was George Snailum's estate agent's office; he is standing in the doorway and the group also includes the Town Crier, wearing his uniform, to the right. Behind, to the left, is Court House and, to the right, a building shown from the other end in the picture on p. 34.

The next four pictures show No. 36 Fore Street, one as the background to a charming pair of flower girls. The lower picture shows how it was used as two shops, Stuckeys, grocers, and Nelsons, butchers, the third (top right) how it looked from Fore Street around 1906, and the fourth (bottom right) from the rear, in about 1906.

Trowbridge, Town Hall

Trowbridge, Town Hall and Market Place

This shows the buildings blocking the roadway from the Castle Street side when they were up for sale, c. 1897. They were bought to provide a site for the Victoria Institute. By that time Snailum's office had gone; he built new premises in Church Street in 1892, so there was now a narrow road through.

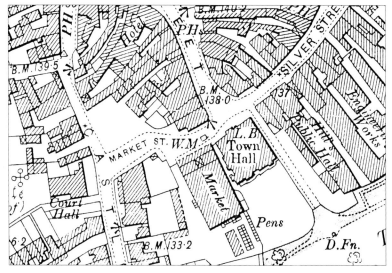

This brings us to the Ordnance Survey 2nd edition 25 inches to the mile map of 1899 which shows a blank where the Victoria Institute was being built. The new street was crooked because of the way in which the garden of Court House stuck out on one side and because of the presence of No. 36 Fore Street on the other. Note also the curved boundary just above the 'ST' of Market Street.

Complaints about the awkward position of this Fore Street building led to its demolition in 1906. These photographs must have been taken immediately to show the improvement in the line of road. In the top picture the road where the house stood has not been made up. In the lower one the scaffolding shows where the end wall of No. 35 Fore Street is being made good. Notice at the left the wall marking the curved boundary shown on the Ordnance Survey map of 1899.

By the time this picture was taken, probably just before the First World War, a new ladies' lavatory had been built at the entrance to the Market Yard, and a hedge had grown on the curved boundary. The exact function of the curved hydrant in the foreground is not known.

Around 1930 someone saw that the curved plot of land had more economic use as a shop site rather than a garden, and so appeared Smetham's card and toy shop: a veritable Aladdin's Cave for younger Trowbridgians.

In 1936 the building at the corner of Fore Street, No. 35, was mostly demolished and replaced by a new building for the International Stores, a national chain of grocery shops. Mainly by some quirk of property ownership, a little piece of the old building survived at the right hand side, and remained for many years one of the town's architectural oddities. Fore Street Garages had a way through to Market Street, for a notice 'Garage' can be seen just above the bus, but Smetham's occupied the shop on the curved boundary for several years more.

In these pictures from the 1950s, Smetham's has been replaced by Hebden Knee Motors. Also seen is the ladies' lavatory and the sign for 'gentlemen' pointing to the site between the Town Hall and the Market House. These latter were replaced by more palatial ones in 1961, which in their turn disappeared when Castle Place was made. Opposite is the unfinished side of the Victoria Institute and the tin hut which, in 1961, the Town Council tried to get removed as an eyesore. Both have now gone but the curved boundary persists as the side entrance to Boots.

Two

Trades and Industries

The woollen industry was the most important source of employment and income for several centuries. Many pictures of it have been published in other books but we believe this to be unpublished until now. It shows the long-vanished factory at Upton Lovell near Warminster, and is relevant here because many workers from it moved to Trowbridge when Hewitts moved their trade to Innox Mill in 1876.

The date of the fire which occasioned this photograph is not known, but it gives us an excellent view of the centre part of Brown and Palmer's Courts Mill in the late Victorian period. The building looks undamaged but it must have been quite a fire to make it necessary for the Melksham engine to attend.

These two pictures show the same building – one on the occasion of the visit of Queen Mary to the factory, then Palmer and Mackays during the Second World War, the other, below, in the hands of the demolition men in 1968.

W. DYER,

BAKER,

THE HALVE, TROWBRIDGE,

Respectfully informs the Gentry, and Public generally of Trowbridge and its Vicinity, that he has commenced business as above, and being determined to use Flour of the first-rate quality, and to pay the strictest attention to the making of his Bread, he feels confident that no other House in the Town will excel him; and he therefore respectfully solicits their favor and support.

Cottage, Brown, and every variety of Bread, to order.

Householders' Bread baked every day at Three o' Clock.

BEST RADSTOCK COALS

CONSTANTLY ON SALE AT THE LOWEST PRICES.

These trade cards are both of the same date, 1852, but it is not known if the W. Dyer who was starting business as a baker (and also sold coal) was the man who had been clipping horses for several years past. The reference to householders' bread must mean that he would bake dough which had been prepared at home.

W. & H. DYER,

THE HALVE, TROWBRIDGE,

In returning their sincere thanks to the Nobility, Clergy, and Gentry of Trowbridge and its Vicinity, for the many favors they have received for several years past, as

CLIPPERS OF HORSES,

and beg to inform them that they intend continuing the same during the ensuing season, and solicit a continuance of their favors.

Gentlemen's Horses attended at their own Stables.

HORSES BROKE TO SADDLE AND HARNESS.

Trowbridge, 25th October, 1852.

POTATOES — SOUTHWICK, TROWBRIDGE, WILTS.

GAIN FROM 2 CWT SULPHATE OF POTASH: 5 TONS 8 CWT OF POTATOES.

This advertisement for Kainit sulphate of potash fertlizer appeared in postcard form in 1907. Presumably the improvident grower who used no manure was too ashamed to be photographed.

SUNDAY-SCHOOL

SEPTEMBER

Anniversary of the Birth-Day of R. Raikes, Esq.

JUBILEE,

14th, 1831.

the Founder of Sunday-Schools.

This Paper is presented to *Fredrick Page* for good behaviour; and it is hoped that it will be carefully preserved, that at some distant period it may recall the happy time when a Jubilee was celebrated throughout the British Isles, in commemoration of the establishing of Sunday-Schools.

John Diplock printed this souvenir of the Sunday School Jubilee of 1831, and this copy has actually survived to some distant period.

43

One of the major employers of the first part of the twentieth century was the Wilts United Dairies, later to become Unigate. The secretaries of the company are pictured outside the Bythesea Road offices in the 1920s.

Workers from the Wiltshire Rug Company, Court Street, c. 1916. Among those pictured are Ivy Usher, Blanche Erwin, Beat Parfitt, Mabel Caroline Rose, ? Vince, ? Watley, Edie Hurn, Elsie Hurn, Daisy Brewer, Lily Brewer, Elsie Parr, Winnie Parr and ? Hurn. It would appear that this group were posed at the back of Houlton's photographic studios in Fore Street.

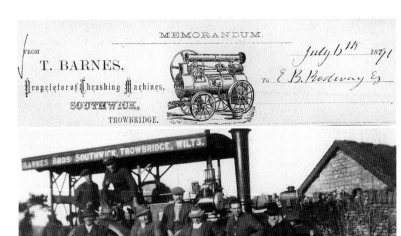

MEMORANDUM.

FROM

T. BARNES,

Proprietor of Thrashing Machines,

SOUTHWICK,

TROWBRIDGE.

July 15th 1891

To *E. B. Rodway Esq*

The 1891 bill heading suggests that Thomas Barnes's business was then as an agricultural contractor, but later the emphasis was on road maintenance, and the firm's steamrollers could be seen all over the south of England.

THE WILTSHIRE STEAM ROLLER DEPOT.

PROPRIETOR:

THOMAS BARNES,

Engineer & Contractor,

Established 1867.

SOUTHWICK, TROWBRIDGE, WILTS.

(Within Two Miles of Trowbridge Railway Station.)

CONTRACTOR
TO THE
WILTS COUNTY
AND OTHER
COUNCILS.

TERMS
FOR DISTRICT
COUNCILS ON
APPLICATION.

ENGINEERING
IN
ALL ITS
BRANCHES.

32 YEARS
PRACTICAL
EXPERIENCE.

THE ABOVE REPRESENTS A PORTION OF THE WILTSHIRE STEAM ROLLER DEPOT, WHERE THE LARGEST STOCK OF SECOND-HAND AGRICULTURAL AND OTHER MACHINERY IN THE WEST OF ENGLAND MAY ALWAYS BE SEEN, COMPRISING ROLLERS, TRACTION ENGINES, ROAD ROLLERS, PORTABLE ENGINES, SEMI-PORTABLE ENGINES, TRACTION WAGONS, THRESHING MACHINES, ELEVATORS, CHAFF-CUTTERS, TRAVELLING VANS, MORTAR MILLS, STONE BREAKERS, CONTRACTORS' PLANT, ETC.

Hadens started in Trowbridge in 1816 as general engineers and millwrights, but soon became specialists as heating engineers. The main factory is still standing in Silver Street, now occupied by Colborne Trophies. Three of these views show its interior, one while converted for munitions work in the First World War. The fourth shows the interior of the foundry in Bythesea Road (*TIP* 43 and 44).

This rooftop view was taken when the chimney at the recently closed Innox Mill of Kemp and Hewitt was being demolished in the mid 1950s. This provided an excellent opportunity for a photographer with a good head for heights to photograph the southern part of the town. In the lower left corner is a former malt house which is still there. It was here that the two maltsters, below, worked around the 1880s.

Another view, of maltsters actually at work, dates from the 1950s. At that time Ushers Brewery had their own maltings in what was then Gasworks Lane, now 'Riverway'.

Beatrix Potter's Tailor of Gloucester sat 'cross-legged on a table', though her picture in the book hardly shows a table. However Trowbridge's William Collett is definitely on a table and in the correct posture. He ran his business from No. 6 Hill Street, which was demolished for the building of the Old County Offices in 1913, in the 1880s and 1890s.

Two forms of transport used by J. Sainsbury & Co., grocers, steam millers and corn merchants, based at Bridge Mill with their grocery shop at 3 Wicker Hill. Steam lorries were much used in the 1920s in businesses where loads were heavy.

CROWN BOARDS AND QUILTS.

No. 801

No. 803

Crown Boards or Wood Quilts are used in most of the honey producing countries in place of the cloth quilt commonly used in this country. It will last as long as the hive, while calico quilts have to be constantly renewed. One central hole, of such size as to take a Porter Bee Escape in the crown board is usual, but our boards are fitted with two such holes, both covered with a wooden slide. These holes enable the position of the cluster to be more readily seen in winter, and if food is necessary, it can be placed immediately over the cluster. Feeding and treatment for Acarine can be carried out at the same time if required. It provides a bee space over the top of the frames—a great help in wintering the bees as they pass over the top of the frames, in the warmest part of the hive, to fresh stores when needed.

801	Crown Board, W.B.C. size	10/-
802	Crown Board, National size	11/-
803	Glass Quilt with feed hole, W.B.C.	11/6
804	Glass Quilt with ditto, National	12/6
805	Hessian Quilts	1/-
806	Thick Felt Quilts	1/3
811	Extra Strong Canvas Quilts	2/-

QUEEN EXCLUDERS.

807	Zinc Long Slot : 16" x 16" 3/-:	
	16" x 17¼" 3/3 : 18¼" x 18½"	3/6
808	Waldron Wire Excluders :	
	16" x 16" 8/-: 16" x 17¼" 8/9:	9/2
	18¼" x 18½"	9/2
	16½" x 20" (Langstroth)	9/6
	18½" x 20" (Modified Dadant)	10/6
818	Queen Excluder Dummy	5/6

BEE ESCAPES.

No. 810.

809	Porter Escapes, 2-way	each	1/3
810	Porter Escape on Board,		
	W.B.C. size	each	11/6
816	National size	each	11/6
812	Clearing Cones for hive roofs	per pair 8d.: per doz.	6/-
813	Frame Spacers (Teswain) Metal Runner and frame spacer		
	combined. 8, 10 or 11 frames	per pair	10d.
814	Dummy or Division Board	each	2/6
915	Carbolic Cloths in tin container	per set	6/-
916	Hive Tool		6/-
938	Hive Tool—Stainless Steel		8/6
917	Hive Record Cards	per doz. 9d.: per 100	5/-
918	Pipe Cover Cages for pressing on to comb		1/-
913	Bee Brushes		4/6
914	Sovereign Sprayer. 1 pt.		3/6
815	Hive-leg Shoes. Per set of 4		3/6
919	Cuprinol Wood Preservative, Brown.		
	For preserving timber against dry rot and boring beetles, and generally lengthening its life. When thoroughly dry can be painted, polished or varnished over and is harmless to plant life. Applied by brush, spray or immersion. 1 pt. 2/3: Qt. 3/9: ½-gall. 6/-: Gall. 10/3: 5 galls. at 9/9 gall.		

COMBINED NUCLEUS HIVE and TRAVELLING BOX, Improved Pattern.

901

A great advance in this type of Travelling Box. The body and cover (with patent fasteners) will hold a 6 frame Stock, or with roof, forms a nucleus hive for 4 frames with a tin lined syrup feeder to occupy the space of 2 frames.

901	Complete	...	50/-

Travelling Box for Bees, with ample ventilation, patent wing nut and bolt fastening for the lid. This Box will meet the demand for a strongly made, easily handled and simple but safe fixing.

923

923	To hold 8 frames	47/6
931	Combined Travelling and Swarm Box, to hold 6 frames	35/-
937	Six Frame Travelling Box	32/6

BEE VEILS.

927	Wire Veil, square folding, copper wire, net surround shaped for shoulders, bound edges	18/6
928	Wire Veil, Round Type, copper wire, bound edges, net surround shaped for shoulders	13/-
929	Cheap Black Net Veil	6/-

BEE FEEDERS.

904	Plastic Feeder (holding 1½ pts. approx.)	7/-
905	Tin Feeder, as above	5/6
906	Bottle Feeder	4/-
907	Spare Bottle	1/6
908	Spare Corks, each	3d.

LARGE SIZE RAPID FEEDERS.

924	5 pt. Aluminium	12/6
936	5½ pt.	14/6
925	6½ pt.	16/-
932	W.B.C. Miller Feeder	18/-
933	NAT. Miller Feeder	18/-
926	4 pt. Lacquered Tin Feeders	7/-

SMOKERS.

909	Straight Nose	9/-
910	Spare Nozzle	1/6
911	Bellows	7/-

AMERICAN PATTERN.

912	Bent Nose Smoker (Tin)	16/-
934	Bent Nose Smoker (Iron)	17/6
935	Bingham Smoker (Large)	30/-

SNELGROVE SWARM CONTROL BOARDS.

930	W.B.C. size	17/-
	National size	13/6

Sainsbury's also sold bee-keeping equipment, a sideline important enough to justify the issue of a sixteen page catalogue in 1948.

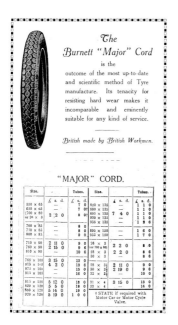
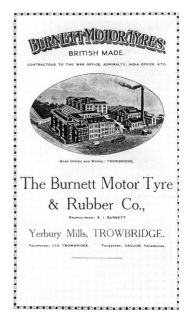

Rubber manufacture has been established in west Wiltshire since the middle of the nineteenth century. Trowbridge first took part in 1915, when the former cloth factory in Yerbury Street was converted for the Burnett Motor Tyre and Rubber Co. The view on the cover of their 1926 catalogue shows the factory greatly exaggerated in size and has 'removed' one side of Yerbury Street so that it can be seen. Shortly afterwards the firm ran into difficulties and was relaunched as the Trowbridge Tyre and Rubber Co. in 1929, and this ceased work in about 1938.

A forgotten Trowbridge industry was the manufacture of bicycles. The firm of Tranter and Morton used part of the Yerbury Street factory to make their penny-farthings, and also had an office and showrooms in Yerbury Street. Tranter, who had been in business for several years, took Morton into partnership in 1881, the year the brochure was issued, but no more is known of the business.

The flammable nature of wool fibres made factory fires a regular occurrence in the recent history of Trowbridge. In August 1931 the Home Mills of Samuel Salter & Co. was gutted by fire. The company continued production as other factories in the town worked up its orders; the mill, less its top storey, was rebuilt and cloth manufacture continued there until 1982 when the woollen industry finally left the town.

Nineteenth-century expansion resulted in a great demand for bricks to build both factories and terraces of houses for factory workers. Brickworks made use of the local clay at Upper Studley, Waterworks Road, and here at Canal Road where the clay beds were worked by the Trowbridge Brick and Pottery Co. in the early twentieth century.

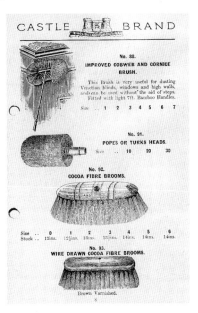

No. 88.
IMPROVED COBWEB AND CORNICE BRUSH.

This Brush is very useful for dusting Venetian blinds, windows and high walls, and can be used without the aid of steps. Fitted with light 7ft. Bamboo Handles.

Size .. 1 2 3 4 5 6 7

No. 91.
POPES OR TURKS HEADS.

Size .. 10 20 30

No. 92.
COCOA FIBRE BROOMS.

Size ..	0	1	2	3	4	5	6
Stock ..	12ins.	12½ins.	13ins.	13½ins.	14ins.	14ins.	14ins.

No. 93.
WIRE DRAWN COCOA FIBRE BROOMS.

Brown Varnished.
8

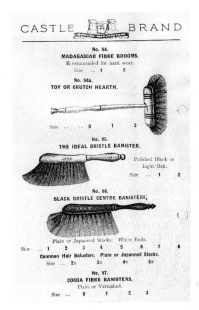

No. 94.
MADAGASCAR FIBRE BROOMS.
Recommended for hard wear.

Size .. 1 2

No. 94a.
TOY OR CRUTCH HEARTH,

Size 0 1 2

No. 95.
THE IDEAL BRISTLE BANISTER.

Polished Black or Light Oak.

Size .. 1 2

No. 96.
BLACK BRISTLE CENTRE BANISTERS;

Plain or Japanned Stocks. White Ends.

Size ..	1	2	3	4	5	6	7	8

Common Hair Balusters. Plain or Japanned Stocks.

Size .. 2x   3x   4x   5x

No. 97.
COCOA FIBRE BANISTERS.
Plain or Varnished.

Size .. 0 1 2 3

Another industry which took advantage of accommodation in a former cloth factory was the manufacture of brushes. J. Avons and Sons used Castle Court Factory in Court Street to make an amazing variety of brushes between 1891 and the Second World War.

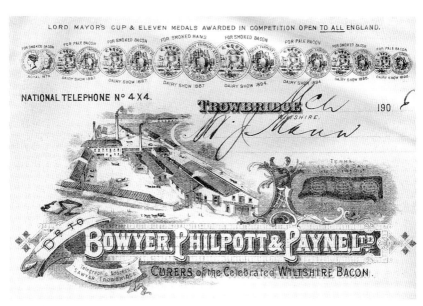

The small factory which served Bowyers until the 1950s is shown on this bill heading of 1906, and can also be seen in the background of a photograph taken around 1958, to show the site of the former Bear Inn, demolished in 1955.

A popular and common view of the Town Hall, but one that is fairly rare in that it shows the shop of Bowyer and Philpot in the open fronted cooked meats shop on the left, which they occupied for only five years, 1893–1898, before joining with Paynes and moving to the other side of the street. The shop was one of several offering similar products but was the only such business to go on to become a major industry in the town. The remaining photographs of local industries were all taken in the 1950s.

For some years after the Second World War, Trowbridge Co-operative Society ran a shoe repairing workshop which did work for many other Co-operative Societies in the west of England.

Inside Ushers in these 1950s photographs we see the processes of bottling and filling wooden barrels. At that time Ushers had their own cooperage to make barrels, but Eastons, shown in the two 1957 pictures to the right, still carried on this ancient craft from a site on the outskirts of the town, Timbrell's Cottages in Bradley Road.

Above, below, and opposite above: At Nestles, Staverton, in the 1950s, milk still came to the factory in churns which were manually emptied to start the process of making the company's Ideal Milk. The other two pictures (below and top right) show that the rest of the process was highly mechanised using a mainly female labour force.

Sainsbury's were manufacturers of animal foods, which were prepared in Bridge Mill, a fine old cloth factory on the opposite bank of the river to Studley Mill. Here sacks of Poultry Rations and Quikpork, for fattening pigs, are being filled while the factory cat looks on.

Airsprung is one of the town's oldest businesses. Started as Chapmans in the late 1870s, it moved from Union Street to the former Stancomb's cloth mill at Cradle Bridge in 1905. After the Second World War the factory expanded into the large building on the opposite side of the river, now occupied by the Wiltshire County Council Library and Heritage headquarters and the Record Office. It was in this building that these views of bed manufacture were taken in 1957.

Perox Engineering had a factory in Mortimer Street in which they made non-ferrous metal castings. One speciality was aluminium spouts for metal tea pots, seen here in 1952.

Sleightholmes is still a well-known business in Trowbridge. Before its move to larger premises in Frome Road in 1963 it operated from a site in Newtown near the top of Mortimer Street, dealing in motor bikes. This display of 1953 also gives a vignette view of Harry Cleveland's butchers shop in the little building which still stands across the road.

Tremans, its name taken from the fact that it was started by three men, was a firm which specialised in sheet metal work for ventilating systems. The works, still standing derelict at the time of writing, was at the lower end of Court Street.

Three

Shops and Markets

The shop of Caines and Son at 38 Roundstone Street stocked everything a gentleman could need in the way of tailoring and outfitting. It was an example of many small shops in the early twentieth century which provided its customers with a very wide range of stock in a small market town.

Trowbridge market dates from the twelfth century and for many hundreds of years it occupied the Market Place in front of the main entrance to Trowbridge Castle, now near the entrance to The Shires at the top of Castle Street. In the nineteenth century, it moved to the Market Yard between Castle Street and the Park. Bob Hallam's photograph album of 1904 provides a splendid series of the market being held in the Market Yard, on a Tuesday. The Yard is now covered by the present market and the multi-storey car park. The livestock market mainly comprised cattle, sheep, pigs and poultry of all descriptions and the catchment area included Westbury, Bradford and Melksham.

19. SILVER STREET & 52. CHURCH STREET,

Mess.rs Mann & Rodway Trowbridge Xmas 1884
Solicitors, Union street

Bought of W.m G. Parriss,

Furnishing and Builders' Ironmonger.

AGENT FOR

MILNERS'

RENOWNED

FIRE & THIEF RESISTING

SAFES

SOLE AGENT

FOR

HOWARTHS

TOOLS.

OILS & COLORS.

This corner, now occupied by the Halifax Building Society, was known as Parriss's Corner from the long standing ironmongers shop shown here. It was not, however, old fashioned; when the photograph was taken in the 1930s the signs said 'Radio Corner' and 'The House for Wireless'. The fine old shop front with its fluted pillars was a sad loss to the town.

This building can be seen at the right in the last picture when it had a more modern shop front and was used as a cycle shop. In this older picture it still had its early nineteenth century bow front shop windows, and formed part of Parriss's shop adjoining. It was built in 1725.

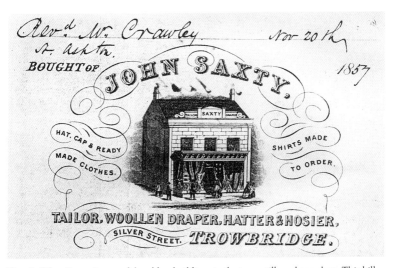

Rev.d Mr. Crawley, St. Ashton. Nov 20th 1857

BOUGHT OF **JOHN SAXTY,**

HAT, CAP & READY MADE CLOTHES.

SHIRTS MADE TO ORDER.

TAILOR, WOOLLEN DRAPER, HATTER & HOSIER, SILVER STREET, **TROWBRIDGE.**

Pitts, in Silver Street, is one of the oldest buildings in the town still used as a shop. This bill heading of 1857 shows it when used by John Saxty, a member of a family with widespread business interests at the time, as publicans, tailors and drapers, and hairdressers. The reference to ready-made clothes is interesting; they were comparatively new at the time as most were still made to measure.

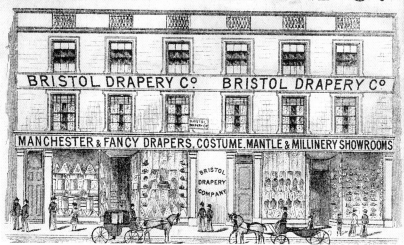

FROM THE 23 & 24, SILVER STREET, TROWBRIDGE.

BRISTOL DRAPERY Co.

BRISTOL DRAPERY Co.   BRISTOL DRAPERY Co.

MANCHESTER & FANCY DRAPERS. COSTUME. MANTLE & MILLINERY SHOWROOMS

BRISTOL DRAPERY COMPANY

Edgar Fear Hill moved from Bristol to Trowbridge in 1880, naming his shop The Bristol Drapery, in the building in Silver Street occupied until recently by the TSB and the adjoining one, now Alms House.

In 1920 the business, by then known as Fear Hills, moved across the street to what had been for many years an ironmongers shop, now Mackays. The new store had its entrances well set back so that window shopping could be done under cover on wet days, as here in the 1950s.

This new store gave much more space since it included the large hall behind, Hill's Hall, which had been the town's main public hall in Victorian times. Fear Hills grew into a departmental store selling china, furniture and household goods as well as drapery. Above is a busy Christmas scene. The store always had its own Father Christmas, in the drapery section at the front of the shop; below is the furniture display in the large hall on the upper floor. Both pictures are from about 1957.

Roberts's grocers shop and the Mortimer Street Post Office were modern buildings when this view was taken, around 1908; they were built when Bythesea Road was made a few years earlier. Across the road to the left are the Foundry Fields, later to become the Trowbridge Town football ground and, later still in 1939, the site of County Hall. Beyond are the two villas, still standing near the Drill Hall, and Haden's Foundry.

Eli B. Cantello's cobblers shop stood in a row of houses which stretched along Newtown from near the corner of Gloucester Road, a site now occupied by advertisement hoardings. He was in business with his son until the start of the First World War.

Henry Sims was in business as a music seller in Hill Street, facing the Town Bridge, by 1888, and by 1897 had added a bicycle business. This was a time when cycling was booming owing to the introduction of the safety bicycle, as shown in this picture, which superseded the older, and more dangerous penny-farthings. After the First World War motor cycles were also sold.

Many inland towns had a business described as a marine store. That of William Pike was at 1 Shails Lane, in the 1920s, facing along Hill Street. He also had premises at Innox Mill.

The business of A. Davis & Son, greengrocer and fishmonger, was established in 1895. In 1910 Charlie Davis, his wife, Alice, and two daughters, Bessie and Winnie, were pictured outside the shop at 2 Church Walk. The tankard on the fish display was doubtless used for selling shellfish and shrimps by the pint.

Church Walk has contained shops with living accommodation above for well over a century. A good range of shop fronts in 1907 included: No. 1, Trowbridge Co-operative Industrial & Provident Society; No. 2, Albert Davis, greengrocery and fish; No. 3, Herbert Jenkins, newsagent; No. 4, Alma White, confectioner; No. 5, Albert Young, confectioner; No. 6, Albert Young, fruiterer; No. 7, Bowyer Philpot & Payne; No. 8, Purnell & Sons, tailors; No. 10, Frank Hilser, jeweller; Nos. 12 and 13, Albert Taylor, drapers. The gabled building at the far end is the back of the ancient timber-framed building which housed Knee's Corner Store until demolition in 1936.

W.H. Sims began his business in Roundstone Street, and later also at 12 Church Street. He was not at Nos. 9 and 10 Church Street, as shown in the photograph, until about 1890. Earlier this building had been used by George Hanks, umbrella, parasol, patten, clog and trunk maker, who was there around 1850, and later by William Bath, umbrella and trunk maker. The umbrella trade was continued during the Sims ownership; after the stone tile roof shown here was replaced by pantiles, the words, 'Ye Olde Umbrella Shoppe', were painted on the tiles in Gothic letters.

G. HANKS,
UMBRELLA, PARASOL,
PATTEN, CLOG,
AND
TRUNK MAKER,
BACK-STREET, TROWBRIDGE.

Most of these buildings in Fore Street in 1910 are little changed although their uses may have altered considerably. The butchers shop of the Garlick brothers is prominent, as is the department store of H.J. Knee, which has been in the centre of Trowbridge shopping since 1886. Other shops visible in this commercial area include a bakery, a drapers and a chemist

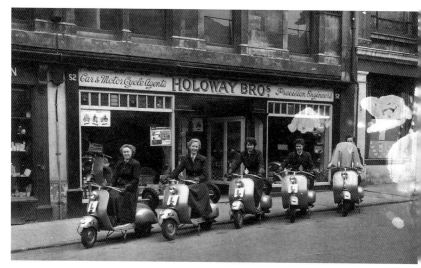

Holloway Brothers' shop was in Stallard Street, in the building presently occupied by 'Junk and Disorderly'. This 1953 photograph shows a row of newly-introduced scooters with what are probably their new owners astride them.

Four

By Road and Rail

In the early and mid-twentieth century, most freight was still carried by rail, although road transport was making inroads into what was a near monopoly in the nineteenth century. E.F. Hillman's lorry, carrying sacks of grain, is pictured outside the New Inn, now the site of the Co-op Store, in Silver Street.

Trowbridge Railway Station.

July 19th 1905 - B.L.B.

The Great Western Railway Station, built to a Brunel design, was a great asset to the town, providing access to efficient transport for Trowbridge manufacturers and trades people. Raw materials including coal, and items not made or grown locally, were brought in while manufactures were exported. It was also the starting point for holiday outings to Weymouth. The large staff in 1905 were under the station master, William Wilcox.

Almost at the end of the steam era, GWR No. 7808 Cookham Manor stands in Trowbridge Station in 1964. To the left, sidings still occupy the area now used for car parking.

A NEW MOTOR FAMILY SOCIABLE. NOW BUILDING.
MAY BE SEEN RUNNING IN TROWBRIDGE NEXT YEAR.

No doubt the first motor seen in Trowbridge, this piece of what was then not far short of science fiction, appeared in *King's Quarterly*, a magazine published by Edgar King. He was the owner of King's Varieties, a toy and fancy shop in the premises now occupied by Dorothy Perkins.

This accident happened on 10 January 1923, when an Ushers four-ton Sentinel steam lorry demolished the wall on the upper side of the Town Bridge and nose dived in to the river. Luckily the rear wheels stuck in the roadway, so the driver and his mate were able to scramble out of the cab unhurt; a man riding on the back of the lorry jumped clear.

Three methods of delivering milk from the inter war years. The two-wheeled cart with its shining churn, from which milk was drawn into a smaller can and then delivered into the customer's milk jugs, was still a familiar sight. Trowbridge Co-operative Society pioneered the sale of bottled pasteurised milk from its model dairy at the top of Court Street.

The delivery vehicle of Ideal Home Furnishers, owned by R.F. Chapman, who had moved their business from Stallard Street to 36 and 37 Roundstone Street in the mid-1930s.

Nothing remains of what is shown on this picture, taken in the mid-1930s to show Ernest Dennis's array of Ford vehicles, including two Fordson tractors on the lorry. Dennis had recently taken over Rutland House to extend his motor business from Castle Street. The rest of the buildings formed part of the Barracks, at the corner of Bradley and Frome Roads. Notice also the errand boy with his bicycle and the man delivering bottled milk. The man nearest the camera wears plus-fours, then a popular item of clothing not limited to the golf course.

Are floods a thing of the past in Trowbridge? They are certainly much less frequent since the improvements to the river in recent years, before which it overflowed regularly at Cradle Bridge and less often at the Town Bridge. But who knows what would happen if we had rainfall which produced the two greatest floods of modern times, as shown here? The 1894 picture (top) shows Hill Street under water while in the 1960 one below, the water is up to the Lamb in Mortimer Street.

This old-fashioned velocipede was ridden by a member of the Wilkins family, photographed behind the house now occupied by Barclays Bank. So too is the safety bicycle photographed in the same place some years later at the close of the nineteenth century, when the rockery under the window had been cleared away.

The cycling craze of the 1890s is also illustrated by this group pictured behind No. 13 Hill Street. The ladies' costumes make no concession to the new sport. The bicycles have a brake only on the front wheel; the back wheel was controlled by the chain, for this was before the free wheel was in use.

Household deliveries and collection of goods from the railway station were made using horse drawn tradesmen's trolleys. On the Down, in 1912, Charlie Davis is pictured at the head of his horse while his daughter, Winnie, holds the reins.

Coach outings to the seaside became popular before the First World War. The picture, taken outside the Tabernacle Church, dates from about 1912. The coach is almost identical to the one which appeared about ten years later on the bill heading of H.F. Barnes of the Town Bridge Garage.

TELEGRAMS :
BARNES, GARAGE.
TROWBRIDGE.

ELEPHONE :
55 TROWBRIDGE.

REFERENC

NO......................

H. F. BARNES,

Town Bridge Garage, Trowbridge, *July 25th* 1922

QUOTATION.

Five

Military Service
and Public Service

From 1887 to 1911 the post office was sited in the lower part of Wicker Hill. The entire staff are pictured around the turn of the century when letters and parcels were delivered in the town at 7.00 and 10.15 a.m. and 1.00 and 6.40 p.m. A letter for London posted before 7.00 a.m. and one for Bristol posted by 5.00 p.m. would both be delivered the same day.

The Barracks, built in 1794, stood on the site at the junction of Bradley Road (to the right in the top picture of 1900) and Frome Road, behind the buildings. The original block consisted of stables below and accommodation for the men above. Behind it can be seen the roof of the later Victorian block. The picture was taken from the front of the house, shown below, which was probably built for the barrack master.

This more familiar view of the Barracks, around 1902, is from the Frome Road side and shows more fully the three storey Victorian block. In 1917 the poet, Edward Thomas, was stationed here for a short time before moving to Codford prior to embarking for France where he met his death at the Battle of Arras. At least two of his poems were written at Trowbridge, which he had known well in more peaceful times and mentions in In Pursuit of Spring.

The Trowbridge Rifle Volunteers appropriately parade outside Parade House, then with a shop window and festooned with creeper in the late nineteenth century.

These scenes date from September 1914, and are believed to show the Trowbridge men of the 4th Wiltshires, the territorial battalion of the regiment, going to Devizes to prepare for embarkation to India. It is curious that many of the men had incomplete uniforms and the whole occasion seems to be, in military terms, a shambles.

A further scene from September 1914 which shows some of the men, their families and friends on The Parade outside Parade House. The attitude of many here seems to reflect the common contemporary view that it would all be over by Christmas, and that there was not too much to worry about.

The 4th battalion of the Wiltshire Regiment had been in camp at Sling Plantation on Salisbury Plain at the outbreak of war in August 1914. Drafts from the depot at Trowbridge soon brought them up to more than full strength and they were to serve in Palestine and Egypt, as well as India. Here they march along Fore Street in front of Foster's and Knee's shops.

These two postcards are captioned, on the back, 'Aussies band' though only some of the men have the Australian slouch hat. In the top picture the band and troops are lined up in the Barracks and in the lower they are marching along Newtown. The troops behind the band have white bands around their caps, indicating that they are officer cadets in training.

British tank No. 222 Mark IV type had taken part in the battles of Arras, Ypres Salient, Messines and Cambrai in 1917. Its presence at Arras and its coming to Trowbridge create a poignant link with Edward Thomas, who had served at both places and died at the former. It was brought to a corner of Trowbridge Park between the war memorial and the Market Yard in December 1919 as a reminder of battles in which local men had fought and died. The tank was broken up for scrap during the Second World War in 1941.

The years after the war always saw a good turn out to honour the fallen of two world wars, as at this Remembrance Day in Trowbridge Park in the 1950s. Some of the children pictured were fathered by men who did not return, while the others were the result of the post-war baby boom. All could play on the slide, swings and roundabout in the Park while their fathers might have jobs in the four remaining woollen factories, one of which, McCalls, is visible in the background. The avenues of Cornish elms eventually succumbed to Dutch elm disease in the 1980s but, until then, were a fine living memorial to Trowbridgians who had died in the war.

NEW OUTFIT OF THE TROWBRIDGE FIRE BRIGADE. 1892.
N. B. COPIES OF THE ABOVE SHOWING THE PORTRAITS MAY BE HAD IN PHOTO FORM OF Mr J. W. CULVERHOUSE
THE PARADE, TROWBRIDGE.

The new uniforms of the Trowbridge Fire Brigade were of great local interest and doubtless many copies of this were purchased from John William Culverhouse, who had begun as a photographer but by 1892, had expanded his business into wines, spirits and tobacco, as well as photographs, at 7 Wicker Hill. The captain of the brigade was William Henry Stanley.

Officers and men of the Trowbridge Fire Brigade at the turn of the century before the splendid facade of the Market House which had been built by William Stancomb in 1861. The fire escape and appliances were housed here.

A drawing of the Trowbridge Free School is in *TIP* 34. Now a photograph has been found, no doubt taken just before its demolition in 1859. The 'blue-coat boy' in the niche was placed there in accordance with the will of Jonathan Reynolds, a carpenter and builder, who died in 1784.

The County Library Service was set up in 1919 and for many years was based at Prospect Place. Pictured outside the headquarters are many of the staff in 1952. From left to right, bottom row seated: Miss Norah Hobbs, Miss Eunice Chapman, Mrs B. Newton, Miss J. Aylett, Miss G.E. Furminer, Miss L.R. Andrews, Miss E. Sutton, Mrs C.A. Phillips, Miss M.L. Payne, Miss M.A. Collier. Middle row: Sid Thomas, Reg Newton, Frederick Hallworth, Miss B. Watts, Miss M.B. Coughlin, Harry Kay, E.W. Davidson, J.D. Todd. Back row: A.W. Shephard, C.c. Ellis, F.J.R. Blissett, R.S. Gowen, V.J. Kite, L.P. Townsend, R.W.D. Stevens.

County Hall was damaged by a fire on 11 January 1958, which destroyed part of the roof and the clock tower. The main losses were of school medical records which had been stored in the roof. The fire started in the early hours and fears that the fire would get out of control prompted volunteers to move motor buses from the Western National depot on the other side of Bythesea Road.

Six

Celebrations, Entertainment and Church Life

By 1937 when the recently opened Regal and New Kinema, both in Bythesea Road, had opened, the town possessed three cinemas. The one in the Market Place, which had been the Picture Palace, was now the Gaumont, and ended its days as the Odeon. It is difficult to assess the impact of Hollywood films on small towns and rural communities in the 1930s but attendances were very large, with many people going every week. This picture shows the opening of the New Kinema.

Above and left: These buildings in Fore Street (top) were decorated for either the laying of the foundation stone, in 1887, of the Town Hall or for its opening, in 1889. Looking to the right, along Manvers Street, we see Foleys Auction Mart on the left. By the time of the parade in Manvers Street, in about 1910, another building had appeared, the motor engineering works of A.A. Bodman.

Opposite below: The erection of this castle entrance, complete with portcullis, on Wicker Hill must have been brought about by a major celebration. A good candidate for this is the Coronation of George V in 1911.

One of the floral arches erected by Hadens, the Trowbridge engineering firm, near the entrance to their works in Silver Street, is shown in *TIP* 111. They were a popular feature of Flower Show celebrations in the 1870s and 1880s. This one shows employees of the firm in the view along Silver Street towards the top of Church Street.

The exact occasion of the celebration in Upper Broad Street in the Conigre is not known; it may well have been Queen Victoria's Jubilee of 1887 or 1897. On the left is the Coach and Horses public house which was licensed from the late eighteenth century until The Conigre was largely cleared in 1934. Even after that the building survived (lower picture) until the 1950s, being used as two houses.

The first Trowbridge Trades and Labour Club and Institute stood on the site of the present one, which replaced it in 1924, in Newtown. The cottage which housed it was earlier called Dunsany Cottage after Lord Dunsany, the defeated Conservative candidate in West Wilts in 1906.

Mrs Ward, the wife of the Labour candidate for West Wilts, lays the foundation stone of the present Labour Club in 1924. In her speech she said that it was the first time in the whole of her life that she could remember a working woman performing such an act. The first Labour government was in power at the time.

The Chairman of the Urban District Council reads the Proclamation of King George V in front of the Town Hall on 10 May 1910. Most major events in the town took place here or on the balcony of the Hall.

There is much interesting detail in this picture of the visit of King George V and Queen Mary in 1917. Note the two elaborate lanterns flanking the door of the Town Hall and the signpost to Bath on the fine cast iron gas lamp. The board on the wall reads 'Who Dies if England Lives. Trowbridge Men who have given their Lives for their Country.' The man standing behind the King is W.H. Long of Rood Ashton, then a member of the War Cabinet. Three cameras are in action, one apparently a cinematograph camera.

The Coronation of King George VI on Wednesday 12 May 1937, was celebrated in great style in Trowbridge as elsewhere. In the afternoon 200 schoolchildren left the Flower Show Field, now Stallards Recreation Ground, and walked along Stallard Street, The Parade and Fore Street to the Park. They carried their Sunday School banners and interwoven decorations in the national colours, and were followed by crowds of parents seen here in Fore Street. In the Park entertainments, music and singing were enjoyed, with 500 under-sevens having their own events in the Town Hall; then all dispersed for a Coronation tea at their schools. Each child received a Coronation mug filled with chocolates.

After the depression of the 1920s there were still many uncertainties about life in the 1930s, including the unsettling episode of the abdication of King Edward VIII. The Coronation of King George VI gave people an opportunity to forget their worries and take part in a nationwide celebration. Many street parties for children were held; this one is in front of the council houses at the top of Studley Rise. All manner of equipment was pressed into service, trestle tables and folding chairs came from a hall or institution but are supplemented with household tables and chairs. Households in neighbouring streets co-operated to provide the food and drink and ensure that the children had a memorable day.

After the railways had killed off most commercial traffic on local canals the Kennet and Avon Canal was frequently used for pleasure trips. Around 1870, members of the Wesleyan Methodist Church assembled at Hilperton Wharf for their annual outing. The coal merchant, Alfred Cox, was in business at the Wharf from the late 1850s to the early 1870s importing coal from the Somerset coal field before this traffic moved to the railways.

The Boys Brigades were seen as good moral and character building organisations. The 1st Trowbridge Company were photographed in the yard of Bridge Mill in about 1905.

These carnival children were pictured in the 1920s in front of No. 62 Dursley Road, then a tiny shop kept by Mrs Shaloe in her front room. Local carnivals provided a rare opportunity for dressing up and excitements out of the ordinary, and were eagerly anticipated.

In the years between the wars Trowbridge Carnival established itself as one of the best in the West Country. In this view, taken from the Town Hall in the 1930s, we see the crowds watching the Saturday evening procession passing along Silver Street.

These three pictures appear in an album labelled 'Trowbridge holiday August 1904'. They show a carnival organized by men in the employ of Ernest Ireland who had been, for some months, in the construction of a sewerage scheme in the town. Led by Kemp & Hewitt's Band, the march started from the Crown in Timbrell Street (where these pictures were taken) and passed through many streets of the town, eventually arriving at a field near the Ship where sports, a comic cricket match and singing competitions were held. Amazingly, the idea had only been mooted earlier in the week, but all the men appeared in costume, each one mentioned in the newspaper report. The upshot was a donation of £25 to the Cottage Hospital, believed to be larger than any single sum ever raised for it before.

SEWAGE SCHEME EMPLOYES ORGANISE A CARNIVAL.

A Record Collection for the Cottage Hospital.

AN EFFORT THAT MIGHT BE REPEATED.

As the result of a carnival, suggested, arranged, and satisfactorily carried out on Saturday afternoon by the men employed under Mr. Ernest Ireland in the construction of a portion of the Trowbridge sewage scheme, a record collection was made in the streets of the town on behalf of the Trowbridge Cottage Hospital. The magnificent sum of £25 was paid into the Bank to the funds of that admirable institution on Monday morning. The men are deserving of high praise for their splendid efforts. The amount realised is said to exceed any sum previously collected in church, chapel, or at any public event on behalf of the hospital. Mr. Ireland's men have been working in the town for a considerable time, yet none of them have happily had to go to the hospital for treatment ; in fact it is their practice to pay a small sum each week to a local medical man to attend any of their number who may be sick. Therefore, the enthusiasm displayed by the employes is all the more creditable.

The following correspondence explains itself :

[COPY].

Sewerage Works Office,
Trowbridge.

W. J. Mann, Esq , Hon. Sec. of the Trowbridge Cottage Hospital.

Dear Sir,—As the result of a Carnival which was organised, and carried out on Saturday last, by the men in my employ on the above works, the sum of £25 was realised. I have, therefore, this day paid a cheque for this amount to the credit of the Hospital Fund, at the Wilts and Dorset Bank. I should like to add that the whole of the arrangements were carried out solely by the men themselves, who also defrayed the working expenses. I am, yours faithfully,

ERNEST IRELAND.

Trowbridge, August 15th.

[COPY.]

Highfield,
16th August, 1904.

Dear Sir,—On behalf of the Committee of our Cottage Hospital I have pleasure in thanking you and your employes for your very kind and successful effort in aid of that institution. The Hospital has been of very great service in alleviating the sufferings of the sick, and it is an exceedingly gratifying incident to find that your men thus render testimony to their appreciation of its advantages. Yours faithfully,

W. J. MANN,

Mr. Ernest Ireland.   Hon. Sec.

"THE HOLLYWOOD" COUNTRY CLUB,
THE GRANGE, Nr. TROWBRIDGE, WILTS. SWIMMING POOL.

The Grange in Victoria Road was converted into the grandly-named Hollywood Country Club in 1938. The enterprise must have come to grief during the war, though The Grange was used as a hotel for a few years after 1945. Evidently the chief attraction of Trowbridge was that it was close to Somerset.

HCC

SECRETARY:
SIDNEY G. FOX.
COUNTRY CLUB MANAGER:
MAURICE H. ZELTZER.
TELEPHONE : TROWBRIDGE 220.

LONDON OFFICE:
99 FORBURG ROAD
LONDON, N. 16.
CLISSOLD 5809.

Hollywood Country Club
'On the Borders of Somerset'
THE   GRANGE
TROWBRIDGE
WILTS

The park provided a variety of sports and entertainment; after the end of the season in October 1937 it was decided that the bowling green needed re-levelling. As a preliminary to this the turf was stripped, first being cut into squares by a knife fastened in a withy branch.

The boating lake in the lower Park was a popular venue for both boating and paddling. In 1955, radio-controlled model boats are being tested on its waters. In the background are some of the buildings of Courts Mill.

The West Wilts Agricultural Show, held either at Melksham or on the road from Trowbridge to Hilperton, was an important event in local farming life in the 1950s. This was Knee's stand at the show of 1959.

In 1937, the Bath and West Show Committee had, for the first time, accepted an invitation from an urban authority to stage their show. This took place between 26–29 May on a 60 acre site at Paxcroft. The opening was performed by Trowbridge UDC Chairman, F. Perkins Garlick, and visitors included the Duke of Kent, who was driven from the railway station through gaily decorated streets to the show ground. The Duke met Nigerian Prince Ademolall, Alake of Abeokeuta, who toured the show with his entourage.

This tableau in the Carnival of 1938 may have been topical – is the camera supposed to be recording the Carnival Queen and her attendants for the new fangled television?

This float must have been made, no doubt by a group from North Bradley, for the Carnival of 1925 or 1926. Late in 1925 the Trowbridge Urban District Council prepared a petition for submission to the Privy Council asking for the grant of a charter conferring borough status on the town. This lengthy document contained sixty-three clauses giving every possible reason why Trowbridge should become a borough, but no grant was forthcoming.

The Trowbridge Operatic Society staged *The Geisha* at the Town Hall in 1937. The cast are pictured on the impressive staircase of that building.

The interior of the Market Hall in use for a flower show in 1955. This gives a good view of the fine ironwork of the roof, supplied by Stothert and Pitt of Bath, when the building was erected in 1861.

'This is our Fifteenth Anniversary Week' says the notice at The Gaumont, so this picture was taken in 1952. The site, now the Fore Street entrance to Knee's, was occupied by the Palace Cinema, the town's first, from 1914 to 1937, then by The Gaumont, from 1962 called The Odeon, until its closure in 1971. The picture also gives a good view of the old building adjoining which was Saxty's hairdressers.

It is hard for young people today to realize how largely the cinemas figured in the social life of the town before television. The foyer of The Gaumont, shown here, would have been familiar to the great majority of the town's inhabitants, as would those of The Regal and the New Kinema, both in Bythesea Road.

In 1803, Thomas Hilliker was executed for his alleged part in the burning of Littleton Mill at Semington. He was widely believed to be innocent and his body, brought from Salisbury to Trowbridge, was met outside the town by a large number of girls dressed in white, and brought into the churchyard before an immense crowd. In the 1960s, a church festival and pageant based a pavane on the death of an Infanta, on this local event in the churchyard.

Trowbridge High School was built in 1890 at a cost of £3,500 and enlarged, at a cost of £1,000 in 1897 for eighty boys, including thirty-five boarders. The football team of 1899 is pictured with an assistant master.

The 1939/1940 football season saw Trowbridge Town become Western League champions. Team captain Bert Blake received the cup from Chairman of the Western League, Mr A.C. Chappelle, at the end of a friendly game against an Army XI on 4 May 1940. Despite the Army fielding several Football League professionals, Trowbridge were winners by seven goals to nil on their Frome Road ground. Players receiving medals were, Blythe, R. Gunstone, Newbury, Jesse Hansford, Bert Blake, Coleman, Newman, Powell, Prentice, Kenny Abrahams and Hunt

A good view of the Parish Church of St James from Union Street in 1905, shows the decorative iron railings which were to disappear during the scrap metal collections of the Second World War. The widened street here had been brought about during the ministry of the Revd John David Hastings who repaired the church, was instrumental in building a new school and almshouses and cleared the churchyard. As part of the latter process he provided a strip of the churchyard to widen Church Street.

In 1934 the peal of bells at St James's Church were recast, increased from ten to twelve and rehung. A fund raising campaign was organised and each bell adopted by an individual, organisation or business. The Usher family were greatly involved and named their newly opened public house, The Twelve Bells. The bells were cast and restored by John Taylor of Loughborough and brought back to the town on a bright sunny day, giving the town the honour of being the first in the county with a peal of twelve bells.

The Boys Brigade preceded the Boy Scouts in the field of organised activity for boys; there was a company in Trowbridge by 1902. Boys had to be between twelve and seventeen years of age, to be members of a Sunday School, and to be total abstainers and non-smokers. They met at Newtown British School. This picture shows them on an outing to Farleigh Castle around 1914.

The impressive Salvation Army Band were photographed in the Town Hall Garden, close to their Citadel at the top of Castle Street, in 1939. For the next six years the Salvation Army were to be kept very busy providing sustenance and comfort to many servicemen.

Seven

People of Trowbridge

Most photographs of children show them with adults, on the street or at 'grown up' events. Around 1900 these children from many of the town's prominent families are taking part in a fancy dress party. Several of the children became the next generation of business and professional men in the town.

Roger Thomas Clark, shown here in his volunteer uniform, was senior partner in the woollen manufacturing firm of John and Thomas Clark when the photograph was taken in 1867. In 1876, a fifty-seven year old bachelor, he created a sensation in Trowbridge by marrying Dorcas Pearce, who had worked in his factory. She was twenty-eight years his junior and had been sent away to the home of Dr George Mansfield, a clergyman who had formerly been vicar of Holy Trinity Church here, to be prepared for her new status. The couple never had children. Thomas died in 1899 and Dorcas lived on at Bellefield House until 1938.

DEATH OF MR. WILLIAM PIKE.

Man of Many Trades and a Genius for Business.

Trowbridge lost one of its oldest tradesmen and best-known inhabitants by the death on Monday morning of Mr. William Pike, of 1, Shails Lane, at the age of 84 years. For a period of half-a-century up to a few years ago it is safe to say that everybody in Trowbridge, and many people over a far wider area, knew "Bill" Pike, as he was usually called. He had lived a full life. His beginnings were of the very humblest, he had known dire poverty, and he had dealt in thousands of pounds. He had been by turns bootmaker and coachbuilder, fishmonger and butcher, dealer in everything, metal merchant and vendor of waste of every kind. He had grit and perseverance and great business acumen. He was of the sort from which merchant princes evolve, and had he been born in other spheres none can say what he might have made of his life. His "schooling" was a minus quantity, but if anybody knew how many beans make five that was "Bill" Pike. Trading was in his being, and if everything he touched did not turn to gold he usually made it turn into copper or silver, for he was a shrewd buyer and could teach the moderns a great deal in salesmanship. He believed in a straight deal, and nobody who ever dealt with him could say that he ever went back on a bargain—and sometimes he lost on a deal, of course.

The writer remembers a conversation with him a year or two ago, when he recalled incidents in his varied life. "You know," he said, "I was a bootmaker by trade, and I was pretty good at making boots for cripples—that was my speciality. Up to only a few years ago people used to write to me and ask if I could make cripples' boots to replace some I had made years before, and which had at last worn out. "I'll tell you how I started coach-building. One day I bought an old trap in the Market for five bob. I brought it home and made up my mind I'd mend it and sell it again, but I found I wanted a few pieces of wood—and I hadn't another shilling in the world to buy it. I talked to the missus about it and she went straight to a box and brought out a five-shilling piece. There were not too many shillings in our house in those days, and I didn't know she had this put away—but she gave it to me to buy the wood, I mended the trap and that's how I started. My first workshop was the road, and I got into a bit of trouble over that too, later on—obstructing the highway, they said—but 'Billy' Walker put it right for me."

Forty years ago William Pike was known for miles around as a "maker of carriages for the nobility and gentry," and many a smart pony-chaise did he turn out of his workshops, where he had the help of his sons as they became of working age—which was quite early in their lives.

But while he was a coach-builder, and later a garage proprietor, William Pike was first and foremost a dealer, and perhaps the biggest deals of his life were at the close of the war, when the military camps at Codford and Sutton Veny and other parts of the Plain were dismantled and sold by the Disposals Board. William was

among the biggest buyers, and his bids went up to thousands of pounds, until his "depots" in Trowbridge were chock-ful of material—dozens of aeroplane-wings, hundreds of duck-boards and Army tables, Army huts by the score, waggons and limbers and wheels of all sorts and sizes, chairs and forms, wheelbarrows and water-tanks. What a collection was there! Most of it was re-sold quickly, and skeleton aeroplane wings fencing many a back-garden in the district to this day are mementoes of "Pike's orchard," where almost everything imaginable could be obtained in those days.

Mrs. Pike died in March last at the age of 85 years, and there are five sons and three daughters and numerous grand-children. Four of the sons are engaged in various departments of the extensive family business. Mr. Pike had not of late years of course been quite so active as formerly, but there was never any question as to who was "the boss," and he continued his close oversight almost to the last, being out and about until last week.

The funeral was on Thursday afternoon at the Cemetery, the Rev. J. A. Kennedy (pastor of Conigre Church) officiating. The mourners were : Messrs. W. Pike, Arthur Pike, Bert Pike, Albert Pike (sons), Mr. Herbert Pike (nephew), Mr. Edgar Dallimore and Mr. W. Townsend (sons-in-law). The following employés also attended :—Messrs. J. Francis, B. Applegate, W. Westlake, F. Feltham, J. Watson and L. Cox.

Above: The Long family of Rood Ashton owned very little property in the town, but a great deal near to it, and were much involved in local life. The last member to live at Rood Ashton Hall was Walter Hume Long, who was a politician of note holding a number of ministerial posts before his retirement in 1921. He was the created Viscount Long of Wraxall. Here he is pictured, in the courtyard of his Stable Lodge, with his grandson, David, whose father, Col Walter Long, had been killed in the First World War. David succeeded as Second Viscount on his grandfather's death in 1924.

Left: John Herrington was gamekeeper to Sir Roger Brown and then to his heir, W.J. Mann, on the estate at Brokerswood. He was born in Dorset about 1825.

Born at North Bradley in 1841, John Merrett was a man of many parts. His profession was the law, and he was for many years managing clerk at Collins, Mann and Rodway. He was also company secretary to Bowyers and registrar of marriages. In his spare time he was a pioneer photographer and a lithograph printer, while his mechanical turn of mind resulted in several inventions. These included a kite shaped like a hawk, used by sportsmen when shooting birds, and a paper trimmer which became an essential in photographic studios all over the world.

Willie Fryer lived in one of the cottages near the Dursley Arms shown on page 27. He was almost blind, but managed to deliver the Wiltshire Times from his barrow in Lower Studley.

John Edward Docking, a Cornishman born in 1844, came to Trowbridge in 1870 as a wholesale cloth merchant. For many years he was well known as a politician in the Town and County Councils, gaining a reputation for the outspoken advocacy of his radical views. Among his more extreme gestures were always addressing Lord Bath, then Chairman of the County council, as 'Mr Bath', and having the word 'humble' removed from an address to Queen Victoria.

The wedding of Winifred, daughter of John Merrett, and Clement Smith of Devizes took place at Zion Chapel in 1904, and pictures were taken in the garden of No. 13 Hill Street, the bride's home. Wedding photographs were not regarded as essential in those days, and groups of this kind are limited to the weddings of the better off, and even then were not all that common.

Thomas Kelson is shown here wearing the medals he won in the Crimean War. He was present at the battles of the Alma and Inkerman and at the siege of Sebastopol. When this photograph was taken in 1897, he was the sole survivor of a Company of 108 men of the 7th Royal Fusiliers. Appropriately he lived in Alma Street.

Billy George was the only Trowbridge Town player, so far, to go on to play for England. In 1894 Aston Villa played a Western League XI which included three Trowbridge players. That the Western League won 2 - 0 was largely owing to a superlative display in goal by George, who was an artilleryman stationed at the Barracks. On the strength of his performance he was signed by Aston Villa and played for them for a number of seasons.

The popularity of photography in the 1860s meant that we have pictures of people who were born in the eighteenth century. Here is a man from Trowbridge, born when Louis XVI was still on his throne in France. Richard Rogers was born in 1788 at the New Inn in Silver Street, and kept a tallow chandler's shop in Church Street until his death in 1867.

In October 1939, Trowbridge businessman Albert Davis drove in from Bradford on Avon in his four-wheeled gig pulled by Tommy Lad. Stopping at the Wiltshire Times office in Duke Street, he was photographed outside Duke House. The photograph appeared in the newspaper for 21 October and the caption included the words, '...the shortage of petrol gives the horse a chance to return to the road.' Duke House, basically of the seventeenth century with Georgian additions, was once the home of the Gouldsmith family of clothiers. In the twentieth century, it housed the Garrick working men's club, and later the British Legion Club, before being demolished when Duke Street was extended to join The Halve.

In the days before radio or television huge crowds awaited the declaration of the poll at election time. This is the crowd in front of the Town Hall at the by-election of 1911, when the Hon. Geoffrey Howard held West Wilts for the Liberals by 581 votes.

Captain E.E. Bennett was the first Labour candidate in West Wilts, coming third in the General Election of 1918.

In the days before chain stores invaded towns like Trowbridge, the main shops were run by people well known to their customers, as they supervized their staff themselves. Here are two who must have been very familiar to Trowbridge people in late Victorian times. Ebenezer Chettle (above, with his wife) ran a drapery and outfitter's business in part of the Midland Bank building. It had been founded by his father in 1844, and continued in family ownership until early in the present century. Philip Lawrence Hill, photographed in his smoking cap, began business at the corner of Church Street and Silver Street in 1856, and moved to the premises in Silver Street, now occupied by Sketchleys and Mackays in 1861. His ironmongery business was the largest in the town.